895

100237

AF412519

to the fierce guard
in the Assyrian Saloon

the first book
of poems of Lee Douglas

by
Howard W. Robertson

Ahsahta Press
Boise State University
Boise, Idaho

"the barber did just what I told him," was published in **Yet Another Small Magazine** (Hartford, Conn.: Andrew Mountain Press) v. 2, no. 1 (1983).

Editor for Ahsahta Press: Tom Trusky

Copyright © 1987 by Howard W. Robertson

Library of Congress Catalog Card Number:
86-071904

ISBN 0-916272-33-8

Contents

Introduction

REMEMBERING HOWARD ROBERTSON

Howard Robertson was never perfectly clear to me, and so it is that as I think back upon him after the passage of several years certain things remain vague and undecided in my mind. On the other hand, he becomes much more clear, achieving in my eyes a focus he never had. I am sure this is something I ought to try to explain.

I recall that we sometimes had lunch together in the cafeteria at the California Institute of the Arts, near Los Angeles. This was in the early 1970s. He had come to me by an indirect route, as people come—somebody wants to become a writer, as Howard Robertson did; so somebody who knows the hopeful writer refers him/her to someone who has actually become a writer, on the grounds that the innocent hopeful writer can somehow improve his spiritual situation if only he can sit in the cafeteria awhile with the tried and tested writer and absorb vast quantities of knowledge in a short period. I did the same thing myself more than once so it must be natural.

It was Howard's then mother-in-law who suggested that he see me. Once I met her in the hallway of our art-like college and asked her where she was going and she said, "To watch the boys swim nude." That made an impression on me, but it's all I remember of her. I apologize. Her husband was a liberal member of the Board of Trustees of our school. We had many Trustees, but only a few were liberal, and I was therefore eager to please him, too.

As for Howard, he was working toward the idea of becoming a librarian. That struck me as certainly a sensible thing for a writer to be, partly because of the milieu of books and partly because the work is not profit-seeking. Relieved of the need to sell anything, one has a fair chance of becoming oneself, which appeared to be Howard's intention.

We lunched several times. I think the last time I saw him—not later than 1975—was at his little apartment in Los Angeles, near the University of Southern California, where I was now teaching, having lost my job at the school of the arts. Howard's wife was there, and a child, I believe, and we ate a dinner of fish (I know we didn't eat the child), and I hurried back afterward to my class at U.S.C. and soon out of California.

And so I lost track of his person. He has not even sent me a photograph.

However, I had a favorable impression of him because I saw that he was going on with his writing. Better than his photograph, here came manuscripts over the years, which I read and commented on, and referred to my agent. Thus you can see what I mean when I say that Howard Robertson became both more and less clear to me. As I lost all memory of his features (no photographs) I gained a sense of him as writer (the manuscripts). He was writing work and completing it. He had learned the lesson of the cafeteria—you can do nothing sitting here at this table; you must go home and write your work. He was doing exactly as I had told him to do in the cafeteria at the California Institute of the Arts. I take all the credit. He was going forward. He had no guarantee of anything, no publishers lined up, no agents phoning frantically with deals, nothing to sustain him as a writer, really, besides the library, except the one thing every writer must have: the need to write. Without that need you are nobody as a writer.

Hints are embedded here in **to the fierce guard in the Assyrian Saloon** of the novel Howard Robertson is writing, so enticingly entitled "Dracula's Oregon Divorce," which, he tells me in one of his characteristically long and readable letters, is "funny, horrifying, tightly plotted." I can believe it. Writing poems or novels, Howard has always merged plot, humor, and horror. Plot is the writer's way of seeing life. Alas, that may be how life is. I could do with less horror and more humor in the world, but that's just my opinion, my personal taste, and you can't condemn me for it. My opinion also is that Howard Robertson is a most unusual and worthwhile writer whose work I have enjoyed as I have watched it develop. I think many readers will share my opinion. I wish us all well.

Mark Harris
Tempe, Arizona
September, 1986

to the fierce guard
in the Assyrian Saloon

I picked up that club on the way back in case the neighbors'
dog got crazy which made sense at the time

Anne's lawyer friend had been shot four days before in
downtown Seattle by the husband in a divorce case in daylight
in a broad lobby of a tall office building and she'd just
been to the cathedral where her father had gone far out
of his way to show sympathy for the murderer and then I
had to notice absent-mindedly the gunman was Black I suppose
because I'd been so afraid living in married student housing
at USC but we were calm again just sitting there on the
beach at Whidbey Island where her mother's cabin was the
night before we hit I-5 for the long haul home to New
Geneva in deepest Oregon . . .

    and the moon was rising alone the sea
    whispering like Walt said hoarse and I felt its
    presence pulling archaic under past those
    eighty July degrees and rubber rafts the splashing
    and tanning by my two daughters and their new
    friend and her posh mother the last few days into
    a rhythm of moonpull unlike the coruscated passing of
    rivers more eternal and inhuman and five thousand
    years like this ago or even a couple centuries
    the scattered tribes not having gotten like we
    the upper hand over the dwindling other creatures
    there are so I guess that is civilization so
    complex a web others did and do the dark work
    that we sit safe at midnight where the forest meets
    the sea and then I asked Anne what she thought
    because she obviously was stirring in there and things
    were so hard to pry out of her sometimes but she
    was reluctant to tell though did finally of the
    wondering what was in there in the sea and of
    whether you could see a ghost and the remembering
    when she and her brother Tod who now fishes on
    commercial boats from Puget north to Alaska had
    hooked into something big here that towed the
    boat around awhile until at last it broke the
    line.

I made no move to stop them Susan eight and
Eleanor five being moved last month from the
August clouds this year here to the temperature
there in Sacramento by their mother for a
couple years she says while lovely Anne has
just gone the weekend to try a llama trip
fairly far into the Elkhorn Wilderness in the
volcanic range so young to me thirty six
southeast of here and alone in the apartment
the aloneness kind of lounges in around the
pillows like some kind of very empty place
without precious five and eight year old
daughters and a very so young good friend
that so much memory with I seem to keep
mentioning dad dead a year and a half too
since a month after I finally left Sarah and
the girls because we could not take the fights
any more no matter how much we loved the two
of them or hated each other and there is the
aloneness here and a kind of panic that has
nothing to do with missing anyone at all a
sort of terror at nothing other at all than
just being with no one else to veil the
intense being just there and I gladly would
dust off the old terms from Handy's course on
Literary Existentialism with Handy to explain
or at least schematically describe this an
anxiety a sort of banal excruciation or
something so I go to sleep though it's only
eleven thirty Saturday morning but I need a
nap a dream of not being here of escaping from
monomaniacal monsters I really love and chasing
after fierce lovely midgets I don't care about
at all and this just goes on a long time it
seems when I see a very real sky with pure
white motionless clouds quite a few curling
into the letter ess in the purest most wordless
azure and I wake up and do feel more comfortable
where I am and can't really believe that was
dreaming.

the night I went down during the longest full eclipse of
the moon since 1857(?) to watch it with the tall old guy
in the parking lot who I thought was from Texas but turned
out to be native Fairfield name of McCoy and Bob Stevenson
came down who worked 25 years with dad and has lived in
Geneva Towers since it was built and the two young women
came and set up a telescope and McCoy's wife showed up
and he and Bob had already broke out the binoculars & Anne
came down with the coffee & zucchini bread and so on

I knew something would happen if
I went down there. dad had been
a lot younger than Bob though dead
at 59 a year now. the moon in
eclipse was a dim orange ball dark
on top suspended glowing in space
like a science exhibit or a memory
suspended dim in the mind in time.
Stevenson had hurt his knee hiking
and had to go inside for a minute
for a painkiller. McCoy was still
down there after everyone left.

the barber did just what I told him

---

the way to spot your car in a very big parking
lot at River Valley shopping mall an enormous
place when you've lost a big bright easy to
spot red '71 VW camper in a divorce settlement
and bought a little short brown '82 Honda Civic
four-door sedan that you can't find even though
the lot is not very full is to begin to wander
but immediately bump into Dwight Wong your col-
league at the International Studies Center on
campus and enjoy smiling idly and ask a couple
of cheerful inane questions and refuse to be
impressed by a famous Soviet sculptor who's
coming but be only interested in your own tri-
vial everyday concerns and push this pleasant
vacuity to the point that the car appears from
behind the big fat green Plymouth and you and
Wong laugh delighted that here you are now
director-elect of the center and already making
decisions on the hundred thousand dollar fed-
eral grant for next year and you find your car
like some kind of zen madman or holy Russian
fool or little kid or something.

probably he being a divine and ornery sensei he just
pulled his cowboy hat down over his empty gaze and
ambled off with his sweet smile into the deeper gloaming

---

it was one long sunset from Salt Lake City to Oregon
from right when we took off and flew straight almost
into its beginning with me sitting on the left so I
saw the whole way as it was south a bit until just as
it was finishing the red glow diminishing in the sky
slowly deepening we touched down in New Geneva having
flown so very low over Fairfield on the way in with
everybody's lights down below already on that I could
recognize everything the lumber mill the old neighborhood
the big park by the riverside the old high school the
watertower hill it all really was sort of transfiguring
and very lovely and the whole trip had been that way
or as good in a quieter way with the weather in DC
very fine for October and the annual conference of the
American Association for the Advancement of International
Studies not keeping me from walking all over the Mall
and into everywhere the National Archives the National
Gallery the Hirshhorn the Smithsonian the Library of
Congress the Lincoln Memorial and all the other great
stuff which I hadn't had much chance to see very well
the first time six years ago when I also stayed in the
Capitol Hilton so that walking into that lobby again
I could almost see Lana Waxman from U. Oregon sitting
there or later in the hotel coffee shop Bob McTavish
from Portland State just like it was those years ago
when we three met at the librarian sessions of that
year's AAAIS conference and started the Oregon International
Studies Library Cooperative and held our own meetings
back home and published bibliographies and stayed over
at each other's houses and became good friends until
Lana foolishly left academic librarianship to try a
mid-life career change into she wasn't sure what so
now she does the books temporarily she says for a big
foreign auto repair shop in Seattle and meanwhile Bobby
has become preoccupied keeping track of the secondary
literature on Walter Scott and other purely British
stuff so I don't see them much any more but back then

we were thick as thieves and I went right up to my room
that first time to call Sarah because we were going to
stay married forever and I had to tell her I was all
right and Susan was too young to understand talking on
the phone and Eleanor wasn't even born yet so Sarah and
I just talked like the demons would never come and I
would never file papers on her and she and the girls
would never move to Sacramento where I would visit last
April and take Susan down to see Sutter's Fort and the
Indian Museum behind it with the red-ochre man yelling
with the bottle in a paper bag in one hand at his two
friends not to call him a drunk or he'd whip their ass
and Susan loved the baskets and costumes and beadwork
inside and the redwood canoe with the head and heart
and lungs and liver and kidneys carved on the inside
to make it strong and Eleanor on the way to Raley's
to buy hubba-bubba gum would say she didn't know why
God made the divorce but God made everything so there
must be a good reason but she sure couldn't see any
reason how come so six months later I just walked down
that airport deboarding ramp in New Geneva in the gloaming
and went straight over to see Anne at her high-rise
and she let me put on her tape of the bagpipes playing
"Amazing Grace" and other hymns and curl up on the couch
with her awhile and hug and sort of imagine what one
might hear old boddhisattva say in a spot like this.

the party begins innocently enough the ornaments the
guests hang them on the dying tree the scent of cut
fir changing the room the cheese the cookies bread
and the wine we all eat brought break or swill in the
flow of business of communion of nailing balls panes
robing chains lights tinsel onto the upward green doomed
limbs the paint and glaze bright in amongst the masses
of dark needles and our words in the dim air like scent
bright like more ornaments in a kind of magical way:

    new city budget manager Beth talking to mom
    they're both from Texas and mom's brother-in-
    law in Fairfield chairs the city council and
    Anne of Seattle I just moved in with talks to
    Jim of San Francisco her friend who's nervous
    for his lover silent beside him as pale as cream
    in this white straight room and mom's glad at
    my finding Anne after the divorce and I'm talking
    to Birch my friend since grade school who's
    marrying Nikki that we fought over one night
    there at his place by Walden in the Coast Range
    and the city lights now out the window shining
    from the hills south of New Geneva where Rufe
    Douglas back five generations settled and I'm
    still living here and all the while Nikki's
    kid Craig is hanging back by the walls while
    the grownups chat and eat and decorate and
    daddy is telling uncle Lee about Con Thien
    again quietly you know and I sort of listen
    but intensely enough so he stays after and is
    last leaving with her and Craig who grabs the
    plastic Virgin Mary from the Nativity scene
    on top of the stereo speaker and runs away
    down the hall of the seventh floor from Anne's
    condo and exits by a fire door and scales the
    last six floors to the top where he rears huge
    in the floodlights and screams defiantly and
    Birch and I follow and Birch looks up and just
    shakes his head indulgently and says look at

King Craig up there the crazy fool just like
we were Lee.

---

they call it a quad but really it's more kind of a modern
cliff-dwelling like our very own local version of Mesa
Verde that you climb the ladders of short, steep sections
of stairs spiralling around square, brown corners up
to not a cave or adobe home but this white-walled cell
like our own local version of I'm not sure which secluded
Orthodox monastery on which barren mountaintop in the
Near East or Hellas itself with the monks' cells high
up over the world like this place high up on the third
floor looking out east over the surrounding at most
two-story buildings of the campus area of New Geneva,
Oregon, to see these same hills and mountains as from
Anne's place on the seventh floor now that I stopped
living with her after twelve months but still friends
it's just I couldn't write in her world of lots of
good friends and eating out and seeing plays and going
on group hikes and doing church committee work and watching
favorite TV shows and talking about new movies and seldom
reading anything certainly nothing old or essential
just like it was when I finally couldn't write any more
living with Sarah so I had to divorce her not that I
blame her either of them it's just I need to learn how
not to let a beloved do that to me when she doesn't
even know she does and you can't possibly explain it
to her so it makes any sense and it's a shame because
Sarah was a wonderful, visionary painter and we could
share being artistic types together and we both loved
the two daughters and could share that so I lost all
that and with Anne besides the wonderful, savage fucking
I suppose I liked best the hikes and camping trips to
the Coast or the Cascades like that one last September
with her and her gay friend Jim where we hiked-in eight
steep miles including across creeks without bridges
to Diane Lake and met on the way the three guys from
Spokane with the fishing poles who told us about the
frogs and sure enough as we neared the lake the trail
was covered with thousands of tiny, clumsy, feeble,
swarming frogs and before that the marvelous white fungus
that bled red tears when Jim poked it and I called it

Our Lady of the Fungus shrine and we laughed because
he was a renegade ex-Catholic unbeliever and next day
at the lake the heron rising by surprise off the lake
in the morning and the water beetles dancing their crazy
underwater ballet of circles in the afternoon but Jim
explained everything away whether frogs or fungus or
birds or beetles by the purposefulness of the action
as if that were all there was to it which caused me to
engage him in conversation by the campfire the second
night with the strange moon gibbous and rising across
the lake and the thought of those bear or were they
cougar tracks we'd found in the shore mud that morning
lurking now in the darkness at the edge of the firelight
and despite the rivalry Jim and I had going for Anne's
attention and the fight I'd had with the two of them
the first night because they objected when I peed behind
a log within fifty feet of the lake while they had both
that very same day dived into it to rinse off the trail
grime and sweat which is something they wouldn't even
let you do at a public swimming pool loaded with chlorine
yet the two of us got past all that there in the beautiful,
primeval starlight and discussed the nature of nature
which he thought to be always purposeful yet felt to be
miraculous and didn't put the two together into the mystery
as I believed since I perceived so much gratuitous beauty
to no particular purpose and gratuitous evil for cruel
that such magnificence include the constant, ruthless
snuffing out of lesser by greater amongst all the forest's
creatures plant and animal and stone for I do not believe
natural evil to differ from moral evil since the nature
of the divine nature is revealed as much in either the
human thus not containing appreciably more of it than
the being of Mountain or stand of hundred foot fir or
swarms of absurd, doomed frogs and Jim said I talked
like a book he just read by a mystical naturalist lady
which I took to be a compliment as I believe it was so
we left it at that and he went into his tent leaving
me with nature from the Enlightenment to date is reason
or irrational or deterministic or absurd indifference
or my mystery up until I recalled Walt's advice and by
myself in the mystical moist night air looked up in perfect
silence at the stars awhile then crawled into Anne's
tent and slept and the next afternoon we went back down

and met a group coming up and I told them about the
miracle of the frogs and the little Black kid among
them exclaimed wow and raced on ahead and now here it
is December and I'm alone in my room with my work the
only thing I halfway believe in as a religious observance
and I laugh to remember the one good corny joke Anne
ever told me about how Mrs. Claus never had any children
because Santa only comes once a year.

the day after that week in March when the
weather had been so nice and everything had
started blooming in earnest

Catherine came back in the bedroom with the
news about the traffic light you could see
through the windows of the house next door
where the neighbors were seldom around and
rarely seen whenever they did come home, and
she had observed that from our, I say our because
I was moving in with her on April first and
practically haunted the place even as it was,
that from our kitchen window when you were
standing at the sink you could see through
their bathroom window and through the whole
dim house in the grey morning light and out
some window or other on the other side to the
traffic light at 24th and Henderson which she
stood there long enough to watch turn green
from red and to red again before she came back
to bed with the news and we snuggled up for
a blessed little while.

One of those early
moments on a summer
evening when grace
rings out to true
lovers

---

her stockings were
driving her
bananas Kate
said with
the mineral
water cherry
essence hers
and lime mine
under our
arms on the
way back from
the health
food place
called Genesis
where the lady
behind the
counter laughed
and asked,
"Two long
straws, right?"
as she rang
us out.

London turns out unexpectedly to be a good place to clean
your toothbrush, just sort of stop everything and stand
in one spot and do nothing but use your fingernail to chip
out all the white gunk and dried crud you've let build up
there in the States without finding time to do anything
about it or time even to just go out and buy a new one
for God's sake!
        But then this kind of thing is happening to
me a lot these days since leaving Sarah and with the divorce
long since final, sort of like that lazy thunderstorm over
Moscow last summer that somehow made clear for me, watching
it from the fifth floor of the Hotel Kosmos, just what were
the three main intellectual problems, or subjects rather of
my existence, or sort of like that camping trip to Savage
Creek Falls up the South Fork of the Kalapuya past
Blueridge those few weeks ago with Catherine Howard where
somehow the high forest and the fierce, white water let me
know Cervantes, Rousseau, Hoffmann, Pushkin, Whitman,
Heidegger, and Faulkner were the people some day or other
I had to read absolutely all of in order to think about
Oregon, theodicy, and the Gothic tale.
                                  So that you see, as
a consequence, I know out of all those scrambled eggs I've
so to speak made in that kitchen, or rather getting into
that courtroom, now the destined forms, or yellow and white
lumps, appear, emerge really, from this fluid chaos in the
iron pan, and my divinely scrambled eggs are done, are
finally just so and ready, these the scrambled eggs of my
authentic being!
                And it does surprise me to say that the
first thing I do after I get into my pleasant London room
in the Kingsley Hotel on Bloomsbury Way, which room is my
introduction to the way things tend to be subtly just right
in England, nothing too much, nothing too little, and
better err toward too little if one must err here (though
even as I say this I now recall, as I loafe here in Paris
in the Hotel California near Musée de Cluny, that there is
this great, big, fat contrast between this London, the
tasteful, understated London with its decent intentions

and good humor, and that other London, the world capital
of weird haircuts where tribal madness ambles amok along
every sidewalk, and where I go around insufferably smiling
to myself and saying bizarre and grotesque and literally
fantastic half the time at first, but then I really have
always found too much pleasure in being démodé and perversely
provincial); so anyway, it surprises me that even before
I give supernally lovely Kate, with whom I now share an
address back in New Geneva, Oregon, our first transatlantic
and -continental call, as reclining with the phone in my
hand I simultaneously watch the first cricket game for me
ever, televised or otherwise, England in this instance
losing to the West Indies, and I soon get the hang, if
not the details, of this gentlest amusement which I maintain
definitely derives from this England, the decent, Imperial
one, not that England, the exuberantly absurd, Dickensian
one, and tell her, Catherine, that I made it and it's
fantastic, literally, and that I love her a lot and miss
her already; even before doing that, I'm surprised that
the very first thing I do instead is unpack the toiletry
bag and clean out this blue toothbrush with unexpected
relief.

    These important things all done and the late afternoon
still with us, I stroll down New Oxford Street and have a
chance to bump hard into one of a bunch of glamor punks
who purposely tries to get in my way, and I can feel how
under that fierce garb and savage Mohican he hasn't much
substance really, though one male punk says to a female
punker after I go by that I was lucky, yet no one has moved
a muscle, not even the one I creamed, in fact especially
not him even though his girl friend is looking at him
strangely, but having gotten the ever-recurring juvenile
delinquency out of my system, I settle back down into
middle age and avoid trouble and have a nice stroll, then
eat some, what else?, roast beef and chips with stout
bitter, and watch in the evening a BBC-2 movie called
Middle-Age Spread about jogging, infidelity, alcohol,
aging, and overeating in suburban England.

    The following
morning, my first in England and hot even for July, I
wind up sitting in the Assyrian Saloon of the British
Museum surrounded by the meanest-looking stone friezes
you'll ever want to see, and I'm thinking about the beautiful

Willamette Valley idling between the volcanoes and the
ocean and how it looked from the window of the tiny Horizon
Air turbojet when I flew out, and about how the thing about
cooking scrambled eggs is to know how much to stir and
when to stop, but there's this fierce guard there in the
saloon who asks everyone when they come in, though he
didn't ask me, in a thick African accent why they're there?,
and what are they doing there?, to which the people nonplussed
sort of stammer that, uh, they want to see the stone pictures,
yes, you know, the ancient sculpture, to which the guard
grunts and resumes his immobility and his stony silence,
which causes me to think, in the immortal words of Mae
West concerning God, that he's a living doll, and I really
do kind of like him because he truly belongs where he is,
so I go on daydreaming there a nice, long while before I
get up and move along to the room full of Egyptian mummies
where the pretty, audibly English woman with the bizarre,
red flat-top keeps staring at me, though I never do decide
exactly why.

again I'm astounded how all connects not really
the way one expects or realizes as how strange for
instance to sit by green Charlemagne in front of
Notre Dame with Zolotov at sunset talking there in
Paris this summer about campus politics here in
Oregon whence I'd just flown and he four months ago
on an exchange and we both were happily agreeing
how colleague Dwight Wong would live to be a hundred
because of that bright laughter of his,
                                        or how for
instance in Munich when the monster hailstorm
bashed in cartops and windows and put holes in
airplane wings the evening after the sweltering
afternoon Günther von Schmidt of Bücher Zumwalt
had been telling about the aerial bombing (in
planes made in Seattle and flown by guys like my
dad I remarked in the belief dark ironies were
okay over there) and dad maybe did pilot one of
those B-17's over Munich since that's the kind
of thing he did during the war and strange how
that forty-year-old twin-engine ex-military plane
cruising over the little park on the north side
of Musée de Cluny in the Quartier latin had
somehow made me imagine the horror dad would
never describe to his fascinated sons,
                                        or how I
stayed on the rive gauche in the Hotel California
near the Sorbonne and then finally fixed my tape
deck when I got home so that when I went to pick
up my two young daughters in Sacramento the next
Christmas we listened to the Eagles sing "Hotel
California" a dozen times driving back north on
I-5 and I had to laugh remembering old Théodore
Delarue of Monde du livre opining in Montparnasse
over lunch, after he'd pinched his standing wife's
bottom before our table of seated males, that
American women were like "squi-ri-i-ique" he said
grimacing and twisting his fists in opposite directions
one on top the other but Sarah didn't win she can't

stop me from seeing Susan and Eleanor and now she
has to grant me joint custody and twice as much
visitation the California court says,
                                    or how I walked
past 65 rue Richelieu by chance on the way back
from talking with Madame Avril at the Bibliothèque
nationale and a little blue plaque said Stendhal
had lived there while writing **Le Rouge et le noir**
about which work I'd once presented a paper at a
regional foreign language conference in Las Vegas
after having been urged to the task by Professor
Garnier who ended up dying in spring eighty-one
in his late fifties the same time dad did,
                                        or how
the Andean flute-players in front of the Centre
Pompidou had entranced several dozen of us and a
middle-aged French lady with a flowing scarf had
towards the end begun to dance like something out
of eternity and I'd remembered those enchanted
six months Sarah and I'd had in gringo-haunted
Jalisco when it was just the two of us and we were
in love though next Friday Kate and I move into
the charming two-story and everything's different,
                                                or
how when Zolotov finished telling me all about the
architectural triumph of the medieval facade before
us in the subtlety of the gathering twilight and
after the sublimest session of sweet silent thought
I told him what fascinated me most there on that
square was the manifold private fictions everyone
had followed to come together here from all corners
of the earth and do this fantastical, magical, outrageously
touristical, ineffable thing with one another and that
it was all there, dwelling, latent, invocable in the
power of the word Paris.

---

time is both the healer and the disease is
what Acorn says when I'm visiting him in his
hospital room in Immaculate Heart after the
quintuple bypass and he likes the card I sent
him with the purple and orange starfish on
the wet black rocks and tells me he sent the
same card precisely to his young daughter in
Boston where her mother lives and I think of
my two young daughters with their mother in
the foothills near Sacramento and of when I
met her in Acorn's colleague's Wong's class
those incomprehensible years ago
                        and now Anne
I lived with for a couple years after the
divorce has married a nice boy her own age
and recently mothered a perfect daughter so
I sent her a starfish card before Acorn's
which I sent because I'd liked the one for
her so much with the two big pink starfish
and the little purple one on the rocks with
the oceansurf in the background
                      and Acorn tells
me about the dream he had the night before
the operation where a Black woman scolds him
for telling her she can escape her folk's
story and a white horse comes for him but he
won't mount which brings Mexico oddly to mind
and the women washing clothes on the shore
of Laguna Chapala and the friendly caballero
who went riding with the young American
women
        so I wish Acorn well and leave by the
corridors I left by when dad was dying here
in the same building where I was born and
I sit down a block away at the campus bus
kiosk not waiting for a bus but remembering
how Kate I live with now and her son Nate
and I went the merry three of us for the
second straight year to the tidepools on

the coast near Beulah in a steady April
drizzle to see the many orange and purple
and pink starfish in the dark clear water.

a glimpse into the heart of
time and sex before making
toast

I walked into Ernie's
the night after I
left Sarah and before
meeting Anne pretty drunk
and got pretty drunker
and sitting at the bar
was trying to score
you know, impress the
whatever off some nice
person or other and
forget the middle of
the muddle of the
divorce I was in
so there was she
gracing her stool like
Nefertiti the throne or
Basho's frog her rock
and we got into a
discourse and such and
she agreed to drive
me home but then I
tricked her up into
the Bowdoin rhodies and
stole a sweet kiss
which enraged her only
a little and so forth
O mature and merciful angel!
but just asked me to
cut it out and tell
her where she should
take me which I
did because I really
wasn't a creep but
before we'd left Ernie's
she'd said what even
after I did transgress
the tulips of her mouth

and receive forgiveness
remained as the utterance
of the prophetess, I
hoped:
          "You're gonna please
a few ladies, my friend,
before you're through."

almost good-bye at Haystack Rock

<hr>

I haven't written about her much I realize
now.

I do not blush to say it was love at first sight
the only time ever for me that April at the
welcoming party for her at Emily Gordon's house
and two years eight months later she left with
little Nate in early January to take a better
job in Ohio but there's not much written about
those nearly three years we had which for me
is strange.

We met at the welcoming party in the big white
house and the moment our eyes met we knew though
she would only admit it on rare occasions but
she did she knew we both did at the same moment
the first our eyes met that we were one as if
in some other more ideal world we had always
been one.

We weren't very compatible in this less ideal
world.

The love was so compelling that two months after
meeting I was sleeping more nights at her house
than at my own apartment though sleeping maybe
doesn't exactly cover it but it wasn't until
a year later that she asked me actually to move
in which I did and then seven months later we
moved to the nice two-story white house on Rose
Street where we lived over a year until she got
the offer and took off for Columbus.

Leaving Oregon for Ohio wasn't my idea of a
good idea going against the grain as it does
reversing the trek of the pioneers undoing the
deed of great-great-grandpa Rufe Douglas besides
which having myself been in Columbus one summer
and seen it the idea did not appeal but so

great was my love for Kate I probably would
have gone with her to her better job if things
hadn't been so difficult between us if in fact
it hadn't seemed we'd split up even if she
stayed.

The love we had was so strong and overriding
yet we fought so often and hard about everything
two people living together can fight over like
about who pays how much for what, who gets
how much of the living space, whose kids get
what priority, who does which chores, whose
pictures hang on what wall, whether blue jays
in Oregon should really be called scrub jays,
whether it's bad or good there are more insects
in Pennsylvania where she'd come here from,
whether I showed I cared about her enough,
whether she confused me by wanting to be both
an independent professional woman in a fifty-
fifty relationship and a dependent Southern
belle which she'd been raised to be growing
up affluent in Virginia whose man would cater
to her and be the soul of chivalry, whether
she should tell me when something was bothering
her instead of growing incomprehensibly cold
and resentful and blowing up about it two
weeks later, whether I should stop drinking
alcohol altogether because it turned me into
a brute a Mr. Hyde, and so on we never ran
out of things to feel estranged about which
made life together deeply in love but ever
rubbing each other wrong a slow torture and
Nate didn't help with his intense jealousy
of the attention his mom gave me and his anger
at her for taking him away from his daddy so
that he and I could never get past a certain
point and I have to confess the urge to strangle
was difficult to suppress about the sixteenth
time he interrupted me when I was trying to
tell his mom something and it all kind of almost
came to a head there that end of August last
year after we'd taken my Susan eleven and Eleanor
eight to the Portland airport for the flight

back to Sacramento and ten-year-old Nate was
still out East with his daddy and Kate and I
went to spend a week in the Norseman Motel just
outside of Cannon Beach where we had a second
story room with a view of the surf and Haystack
Rock the third largest monolith in the world
the place where we nearly said good-bye.

The wind was warm off the sea the moon full the
beach magical in the starlight the mountains
like Mexico like Laguna Chapala only thick
and dark with trees and the next day hiking
along Tillamook Head we could see for miles and
the abandoned lighthouse was right in front of
us the one Kate had read a book about and had
told me how dangerous it was to build it or
get a man onto it sitting as it does on a rock
away from shore in the violent waves and it was
there she said she wanted to move out to split
up end it all she couldn't take any more it was
too hard I wanted love the way I needed it not
the way she could give it she said and I said
she polarized the whole thing into our relationship
versus the rest of her life her job child extended
family past future but I cast away all pride and
reason and pleaded with her not to go I'd do
anything not do anything be whatever she wanted
only just please don't leave me and she hadn't
the heart to do it so we just barely didn't
part.

The rest of that week was supernaturally
seamlessly effortless fluid gliding we woke
each morning to the clamor of gulls on the
rooftop outside our window and went into town
to eat where every other place was named after
someone Fred's Food Donnie's Market Elaine's
Gallery Mary's Cafe Bill's Gas and we went
into a few art galleries and strolled on the
beach next to Haystack Rock the striking color
of which turned out to be bird poop and made
the rock best beheld from a distance and gaggles
of kids on rented three-wheel recliner bikes

with bright little flags flapping from high
poles fastened to the seats wandered aimlessly
and joyfully over the eternal beach and we stopped
at the public library where I read about Jean-
Jacques Rousseau in the Durants' **Story of
Civilization** and we climbed Neahkanie Mountain
which was the reason Kate first wanted to come
to Cannon Beach when she read about this mountain
rising straight up from the sea right after she
got to Oregon and over two years later we had
made it just before she would leave as it turned
out and later in the week we drove up to Seaside
and walked along the Prom and to Astoria and
stood on the hilltop in the middle of town from
where we could see the mouth of the Columbia and
Kate was disappointed that the town was not a
more impressive or charming place because she
had fantasized about Astoria and the mouth of
the great Western river ever since U.S. history
classes in high school in Virginia and at night
every night the whole week the moon like over
Santa Fe on the beach in front of our motel and
the wind warm off the ocean like I'd never before
known it to be on the Oregon Coast and one
night we watched oldies on TV Bob Cummings
George and Gracie Allen Dobie Gillis where
Maynard turns into Mr. Hyde and we made the
sweetest love the most complete sex just
as if all the tension had never been and
never would be again.

Two or three days of this existence were
sufficient to render me philosophical I
had climbed Neahkanie not to conquer it
but as a gesture of love for the mountain
the flotsam along the edge of the Pacific
the flow of the world the uncertainty of
events in our lives not destiny versus
freedom but accept destiny consciously to
have freedom to change it Susan had said
she accepted her destiny Sartre said you
are what you do Eleanor said what Frank
Sinatra said dooby dooby doo modern science

climbs the mountain but doesn't love it is
dedicated to serving man not the whole of
Being and there was always death dad was
dead four years now from cancer though
he'd always seemed invincible and that
twenty years ago when I made the doctor do
a biopsy on a tiny not very dark mole because
I was so afraid of death this fragile consciousness
built in the void live towards death and live
truly there is divinity in the world despite
death and evil because I need for there to be
though I have no idea what the truth is and no
way of knowing what it is and even the tiny
things of this week seemed significant and
auspicious and perfect like even how the
instructions on the towel machine in the men's
room at Fred's Food were in English and French
everything conspiring to encourage the exercise
of that spiritual faculty in us that responds
to and creates Bibles Sutras Upanishads Korans
Shaman sayings and other images of the unimaginable.

The week of course ended and we went back to
New Geneva and kept on living together and going
to work together to the University Library where
she was a cataloger and I was a bibliographer
and Nate came back from Pennsylvania and we limped
along together through the fall until December
when the offer from Ohio State came for her twenty
five percent more pay supervisory responsibility
chance for advancement she couldn't refuse
and I didn't try to make her and wouldn't
have even if our relationship had been working
great because I won't stand in the way of the
growth of anyone I love and it was funny how
once she had mailed in her acceptance all the
tension between us went away all the love found
a place in the everyday world like she could
relax because she was sure the love wouldn't
trap her strand her way out here on the Western
rim of the world and I could ignore irritations
because I knew they weren't precedents would
soon be gone and our love was so simple then

so constantly sweet why couldn't it always be
so?

My girls flew up for Christmas like they always
do or at least have always done since the years
ago their mother moved them to Sacramento and
then Auburn and so they got a chance to be with
Kate and little Nate for over a week before we
all left for Ohio or California on the same
morning and all of us exchanged gifts on
Christmas and danced and sang on New Year's
Eve and there were strange signs magical
psychic incidents that said there were forces
disturbed that all this was breaking up like
the way the two hand-painted china cups fell
off the bric-a-brac in my mom's dining room and
broke at the same instant as Nate yelled when
Susan walked in on him by accident in the
bathroom down the hall or how late at night
I saw the weird lights flitting around the
bedroom like ghosts in the house on Rose Street
and Eleanor screamed downstairs where she'd
woken up which she almost never does and said
the window was weird and scared her or how
my key got strangely stuck in my ignition when
Kate went with me to rent my new place in the
southwest hills with the great view and we had
to call the locksmith but there were good signs
too like how the air was clear and clean on New
Year's Day after the violent storm the night
before which ended two weeks of extreme inversion
and terrible air quality or how my new apartment
was number thirteen and I had $77.77 in checking
three days before Kate left or how Kate got the
same message from the **I Ching** four times in a
row that we were doing the right thing which
was hard and it would turn out well if we proceeded
in a spirit of endurance humility and mutual
sympathy and it has it mostly has turned out
well she's very happy in her new job and Nate's
happy he gets to see his daddy more and I'm
much happier and more productive in my new place
which is not far from where great-great-grandpa

Rufe's old cabin was and Susan and Eleanor are
happy they have their very own rooms with their
very own beds in their daddy's very own place
with a pool room a swimming pool a tennis
court and a million dollar view of the city
and the mountains and the whole deal really
is okay like the oracle kept telling us it
would be.

Last weekend I called her Memorial Day weekend
being literal-minded I was remembering and
phoned and we caught up and the magic was
still there the crazy lovely magic that still
defies the facts the impossible circumstances
that still fills our hearts I can feel hers
filling it resonates in her voice suffuses
our hearts with joy and longing the wonderful
stubborn magic that tells us somehow we haven't
yet really said good-bye.

when Emily Gordon asked me out to that
movie it was the call back to life
                              after
almost eleven years with Sarah and almost
three years with Anne and now just ended
the almost three years with Kate I'd been
feeling afraid of the world of women of
any and all entanglements
                              Basil was telling
me he didn't want me sticking his nose into
anyone else's business that he couldn't
get up for it
                then Emily took me to see
Journey to Bountiful and I began to feel
motivated I started jogging again lost
weight reached out to people and Basil
began standing up straight when I talked
to him
        even going to that wedding with Emily
and her girls Nora and Margaret couldn't
scare Basil off
                and even though Emily and I
are just friends waiting to see since she's
mired in the middle of the classic messy
divorce and neither one of us should get
very involved right now still it was she who
breathed the life back into this storm-zapped
body electric of mine
                    and I remember when she
told me on the phone after I said there was
a huge rainbow out my window to hang onto
that rainbow but now there are lots of rainbows
this place is good for rainbows and deer out
the kitchen window a young buck with two
velvety points a doe standing on her hind legs
to eat the wild cherries and I jog with Vuk
and Leylah by the Willamette River and sing
"Good-Night Irene" at the top of my lungs and
make them laugh at this exotic Oregon wild
man and his great notions again.

Howard W. Robertson is a poet, novelist, librarian, and father. Three of his great-great-grandfathers arrived in Eugene City, Oregon, in 1853, two by covered wagon and the other by undetermined means. Mr. Robertson was born in Eugene in 1947 and by some pleasant oversight of destiny has ended up living most of his adult life there. He began writing poetry at the age of seventeen while teaching himself to type, though that was the first and last time he has ever successfully composed on a typewriter. Over the years, he has made many apparently foolish decisions motivated by the need to find his own poetic voice. Receiving two degrees from the University of Oregon and one from USC has failed to open his eyes to the palpably misguided nature of his existence; he persists in believing he is following a straight course of steady development as a writer. Visits to Mexico, Western Europe, and the Soviet Union, and time spent in Colorado and Southern California, have been important experiences for him, but the Oregon experience remains central to his work. His poems are not actually his but rather those of Lee Douglas, who resides in New Geneva, Oregon, together with a number of personages about whom Mr. Robertson and he write. The essential theme of their work is that living is a beautiful and terrible mystery that is best faced with humor, endurance, and love. They are currently working on a novel entitled **Dracula's Oregon Divorce**.

Ahsahta Press
POETRY OF THE WEST

MODERN

*Norman Macleod, *Selected Poems*
Gwendolen Haste, *Selected Poems*
*Peggy Pond Church, *New & Selected Poems*
Haniel Long, *My Seasons*
H. L. Davis, *Selected Poems*
*Hildegarde Flanner, *The Hearkening Eye*
Genevieve Taggard, *To the Natural World*
Hazel Hall, *Selected Poems*
Women Poems of the West: An Anthology
*Thomas Hornsby Ferril, *Anvil of Roses*
*Judson Crews, *The Clock of Moss*
Thomas Hornsby Ferril, *Westering*

CONTEMPORARY

*Marnie Walsh, *A Taste of the Knife*
*Robert Krieger, *Headlands, Rising*
Richard Blessing, *Winter Constellations*
*Carolyne Wright, *Stealing the Children*
Charley John Greasybear, *Songs*
*Conger Beasley, Jr. *Over DeSoto's Bones*
*Susan Strayer Deal, *No Moving Parts*
*Gretel Ehrlich, *To Touch the Water*
*Leo Romero, *Agua Negra*
*David Baker, *Laws of the Land*
*Richard Speakes, *Hannah's Travel*
Dixie Partridge, *Deer in the Haystacks*
Philip St. Clair, *At the Tent of Heaven*
Susan Strayer Deal, *The Dark Is a Door*
Linda Bierds, *Flights of the Harvest-Mare*
Philip St. Clair, *Little-Dog-Of-Iron*
Corrinne Hales, *Underground*
Howard W. Robertson, *to the fierce guard in the Assyrian Saloon*

*Selections from these volumes, read by their authors, are now available on *The Ahsahta Cassette Sampler*.